DAILY
PRAYER

A Modern Guide to
Ancient Practices

Joy Hilley

Published by Dunlavy + Gray

Copyright © 2020 by Joy Fitzgerald Hilley

Published in the United States by Dunlavy + Gray, Houston
www.DunlavyGray.com

Library of Congress Control Number: 2020942592

ISBN: 978-0-9997813-7-1

E-Book ISBN: ISBN: 978-0-9997813-8-8

All scripture quotations are from the New Revised Standard Version Bible, copyright © 1989 National Council of the Churches of Christ in the United States of America. Used by permission. All rights reserved worldwide.

Portions of the Daily Prayer and Daily Eucharist liturgy are excerpted without notation from *The Book of Common Prayer,* which is in the public domain.

The front cover art is *Appearance of Christ to Women,* a modern icon painted by Ivanka Demchuk. Used by permission.

Back cover quote: Philip Schaff, D.D., LL.D., editor, *Nicene and Post-Nicene Fathers, Volume I, The Confessions and Letters of Augustin, With a Sketch of His Life and Work, First Series* (Massachusetts, 2012), page 45

For more Daily Prayer resources, visit JoyHilley.com/Daily-Prayer.

PRINTED IN THE UNITED STATES OF AMERICA
FIRST EDITION

Table of Contents

Introduction

I pray that the God of our Lord Jesus Christ,
the Father of glory, may give you a spirit of wisdom
and revelation as you come to know him, so that,
with the eyes of your heart enlightened,
you may know what is the hope to which he has called you,
what are the riches of his glorious inheritance
among the saints, and what is the immeasurable
greatness of his power for us who believe,
according to the working of his great power.

Ephesians 1:17–19

While I write these introductory remarks, I am listening to an Eastern Orthodox choir sing the Jesus Prayer. "Lord Jesus Christ, Son of God, have mercy on me, a sinner" is repeating on a continuous loop. I find myself humming the captivating, beautiful tune throughout the day and night.

Whether I pray the Jesus Prayer silently or aloud, I inhale on "Lord Jesus Christ, Son of God." I exhale on "have mercy on me, a sinner." This rhythm and act of worship resets my heart, mind, body, and spirit.

I haven't always prayed the Jesus Prayer. Neither have I always had an intentional daily prayer time. The turning point for me was a weekend conference on the power and presence of the Holy Spirit, hosted at the Episcopal church where I was a member. Mary and Bishop David Pytches, members of the Anglican Communion from England, led the conference. They taught about what it means to walk in the Spirit and hear from the Spirit, as well as the Spirit's gifts of tongues, interpretation, prophecy, words of knowledge, and healing. I remember going home after the first session and telling Joe, my husband, that I felt cheated. I was in my late 30s, had attended church all my life, graduated from seminary, served on several church staffs in music and education roles, and had *never* heard teaching like that before.

Joe and I had several conversations about being baptized in the Spirit and praying in tongues in the weeks that followed. As usual,

I wanted details—*how* it worked, what I needed to *do*. Finally, Joe said, "Just open your mouth and start talking. He'll do the rest." I admit, I was underwhelmed by his answer!

With a toddler at home, I rarely had uninterrupted time to myself. But I soon had an opportunity to drive alone from Louisiana to Alabama. As I drove, I prayed and asked the Spirit for the gift of tongues. Remembering Joe's advice, I turned off the radio, opened my mouth, and a wave of sounds flooded the vehicle. For almost three hours, I prayed aloud in my new language. It was as if a dam had burst, and the rushing water could not be contained.

That experience awakened in me a desire to know God more intimately and deeply. The kind of longing that couldn't be satisfied by reading a few paragraphs of a daily devotional or praying scattered prayers throughout the week. I began studying the Scriptures with intensity and purpose—not looking for more information but for him. As I read the Bible, I learned that when particular verses caught my attention, I needed to take note of them. To ask questions of the Spirit about their meaning or why he was highlighting them for me. By asking questions, I entered into a dialogue with the Spirit of God.

To help me remember what I was learning, I started keeping a journal. With the promise from Joe that my journals would be destroyed at my death (yes, I actually made him promise that!), I poured out my heart to God. Questions, doubts, fears, joys, sorrows, promises, hopes, desires. No emotion or thought was off-limits in the journals.

Not only did I study the scriptures but I also began to read about prayer and attended prayer conferences. Most of what I read and heard focused on particular kinds of prayer, including listening, healing, warfare, intercession, deliverance, and contemplation. At the same time, I began attending a weekly prayer service at our church. It was the equivalent of a prayer laboratory—one where we could practice the skills of hearing, seeing, and sensing the Spirit—all within the safety of a loving community.

In the midst of this, our family experienced some very challenging situations and circumstances. On more than one occasion, I found myself in the fetal position, crying out to God. Through the pain, disappointment, and discouragement, I realized how much I needed his new mercies every single day. Of the many lessons I learned during that time, the most significant was that God is faithful.

The crises finally passed, and I could lift my head again. By then, we had relocated to Houston so our daughter could train at Houston Ballet, and I was working at an Episcopal school as the head of marketing and communications. There, I not only crafted their core messages, but I also often wrote prayers, collects, and liturgies for school events and observances. My copy of *The Book of Common Prayer* became worn as I searched it for language befitting the occasions. Although I had memorized the rite for Holy Eucharist years before, I was less familiar with the rites for Morning and Evening Prayer. The more I read them, the more I appreciated their richness and depth. Without realizing it, I began liturgical writing then.

Soon I was asked to teach several Bible studies in Houston. As I described my prayer practices to those ecumenical groups, members asked me to prepare a guide for them. At first I resisted. Then, one day the Spirit urged me to write a book on prayer. I began this manuscript that day.

My prayer is that *Daily Prayer* will be a sacred resource as you seek to find and know him for yourself.

The Art of Praying Daily

Rejoice in the Lord always; again I will say, Rejoice.
Let your gentleness be known to everyone.
The Lord is near. Do not worry about anything,
but in everything by prayer and supplication
with thanksgiving let your requests be made known to God.
And the peace of God, which surpasses all understanding,
will guard your hearts and your minds in Christ Jesus.

Philippians 4:4–7

Having read the introduction, you know that I have been on this prayer journey for a long time. Like me, you may have loved Jesus for decades. Or you may be completely new to the faith. You may have serious doubts about the man from Galilee or be completely confident that he is who he claims to be—or find yourself somewhere in between. Regardless of your experience or lack of experience with Jesus, your relationship with him does not have to be all sorted out before you incorporate the Daily Prayer into your life. You only need a willingness and commitment to pray.

I've assembled enough children's toys and IKEA furniture to know what it's like to jump in without first reading the instructions. If that's your tendency, I urge you to resist! I am confident your experience will be enriched if you take time to read this chapter—to learn the *why* as well as the *how* of each of the Daily Prayer segments. Before we get into the details of the Daily Prayer, though, let's talk about why prayer is necessary.

Why Pray?

When I'm asked why praying is necessary, the questions usually take these forms: *If God is so powerful and can do anything, why do we even have to ask? Why doesn't he see just what needs to be done and do it?*

The simple answer is *relationship*. God longs to be in relationship with you. To walk with you. To talk with you. As astounding as it seems, the God who created the heavens and the earth, who formed us from dust and breathed his own breath into us, desires to be with us. That desire was made flesh in the incarnation of Jesus and was empowered by the gift of the Holy Spirit who lives within every believer. Every part of God—Father, Son, and Holy Spirit—wants an intimate relationship with you. In the same way that you and I get to know one another by talking and spending time with each other, so can we know God more deeply by spending time with him in prayer.

The more complex answer about why we should pray is that he has called us to help bring heaven to earth. He has given us authority through his son, Jesus—and power through the Spirit—to unite with him in the restoration of all things here on earth. By praying and seeking him, we align ourselves with his will and his purpose. That's why Jesus taught us to pray "your kingdom come, your will be done, on earth as it is in heaven."[1] The effective work of the cross and resurrection has begun. That work will not be complete until the Second Coming of Christ. In the interim, we are called to partner with him to bring the kingdom of heaven to earth.

Comprehending that we are called to partner with God shifts our thinking. No longer are we an intermittent petitioner, asking for a favor from an acquaintance. We soon realize he is not a vending machine in the sky, waiting for us to figure out the right combination of coins to put in the slot in hopes of persuading him to act. Instead, he is the God of the universe, who loves us extravagantly and calls us to himself through prayer. There, our inmost being communes with him.

In an essay on prayer, Rabbi Abraham Joshua Heschel wrote, "Prayer is not a stratagem for occasional use, a refuge to resort to now and then. It is rather like an established residence for the innermost self. All things have a home: the bird has a nest, the fox has a hole, the bee has a hive. A soul without prayer is a soul

Joy Hilley

without a home."[2]

Establishing a home within—a sanctuary fit for the King of kings—requires time. The Daily Prayer is a blueprint for helping build your soul's home.

Why the Daily Prayer Method?

Building any home requires not only a blueprint, but also tools, materials, and a willingness to work over a period of time. This book offers a set of tools and access to materials. You must supply the willingness to work.

I recommend using the Daily Prayer for forty days—exactly as it is, without variation. If you want to modify it after that, feel free to do so. Why forty days? Formation takes time. Building a sturdy home begins with a strong foundation. Building your soul's home does too.

Developing a life of prayer does not happen randomly. As you build brick by brick, you soon discover that the purpose of prayer is to be more completely formed into the likeness of Christ Jesus. By praying in the same method day after day, using all the segments of the Daily Prayer, you begin to develop an understanding of God's unchanging character and nature. Your mind is renewed. You find that your willingness and ability to pray are no longer contingent on your feelings. You establish a firm foundation.

Critics of formalized prayer usually cite the scripture that warns against "vain repetitions." Yes, Jesus told his disciples, "When you are praying, do not heap up empty phrases as the Gentiles do; for they think that they will be heard because of their many words."[3] However, there is a vast difference between a pagan's empty phrases and the Jesus follower's repeated use of Sacred Writ.

"Vain repetitions" and "empty phrases" refer to a practice used by pagan worshipers who recited the names of various gods over and over again to guard against offending one of them. They believed that the more they said, the more likely they were to be heard. Jesus assures his followers that the Father already knows what they need before they ask.[4] He then provides his prayer[5] for them to follow. Jesus offers life-giving phrases for them—and us—to pray repeatedly.

Jesus's disciples not only had his example, but those of prophets, poets, and other writers whose words had been formed into prayers and handed down through the ages to the people of God. They continued to pray their familiar prayers, in addition to the prayer Jesus taught them.[6]

Likewise, I believe it is important for us to draw upon other prayers and texts that have been handed down from generation to generation and from multiple traditions. Even if no one else in your family is Christian, you are not alone. As a sister or brother in Christ, you are part of the larger family of God that spans every race, ethnicity, and time in history. Praying the ancient prayers of the faith connects us to our spiritual mothers and fathers and to one another.

What Is Included in the Daily Prayer?

Although each of us is unique, we encounter similar experiences, trials, and temptations.[7] Many of the segments of the Daily Prayer speak to those things we have in common and incorporate ancient prayers, scriptures, and contemporary prayers. Other segments leave room for personal prayer, intercession, and silence—so you can both speak in your own voice and listen for the voice of God.

Joy Hilley

The Daily Prayer is arranged in the following order:

Adoration and Praise;

Jesus Prayer;

Confession of Sin;

Psalm 103;

Prayer for Deliverance and Mercy;

Psalm 23;

Psalm or Proverb Reading;

Gospel Reading;

Nicene Creed;

Preparatory Verses;

Petitions and Intercession for Self;

Prayer for Devotion;

Petitions and Intercession for Family;

Prayer for Mission and Purpose;

Petitions and Intercession for Others;

The Lord's Prayer;

Contemplation—Sitting With Jesus;

New Commandments;

Prayer for Peace;

Breastplate of St. Patrick;

Prayer for Protection;

Prayer for Strength and Power in the Spirit;

Prayer of Thanksgiving;

Kyrie; and

Jesus Prayer.

Each segment has its own purpose and meaning and is intentionally placed in the given order. Each is described in the next
section. Together, they give you a full and complete daily experience with God *and* offer God access to every aspect of your life.

Daily Prayer Segment Descriptions

Adoration and Praise

Beginning your prayer time with adoration and praise sets the tone for everything that follows. Before you pour out your heart to God, worship him.

In the Anglican tradition, as the Holy Eucharist liturgy begins, the celebrant greets the congregation and then says, "Let us give thanks to the Lord our God." The congregation responds, "It is right to give him thanks and praise." The celebrant turns to face the altar table and declares, "It is right, and a good and joyful thing, always and everywhere to give thanks to you, Father Almighty, Creator of heaven and earth."[8]

Rabbi Heschel emphasized the necessity of praise by writing, "The beginning of prayer is praise. . . . First we praise, then we believe."[9]

Praise often is an act of discipline or sacrifice. One that requires us to look beyond ourselves, our needs, and our pain. By giving praise its rightful place in our prayer, we "call forth the promise and presence of the divine."[10]

In the prayer Jesus taught his disciples, the first phrase acknowledges the holiness of God: *hallowed be your name.* Jesus began by recognizing God as holy. We also need to honor the One to whom we are addressing our prayers. Joining our voice with angels, archangels, and the throng of saints here and in heaven amplifies our praise and adoration. It sets our gaze higher. The words of adoration and praise in the Daily Prayer are taken from Revelation, various psalms, and *The Book of Common Prayer*.

Our God is King of kings and Lord of lords. He is worthy of all praise. Offering him praise and adoration is an act of worship. In doing so, we recall his vast love, grace, mercy, power, and faithfulness. That gives us confidence in his ability and willingness to

move on our behalf—before we begin the petition and intercession sections of the Daily Prayer.

Jesus Prayer

Borrowing from the Eastern Orthodox church tradition, next
we pray twelve words: *Lord Jesus Christ, Son of God, have mercy on
me, a sinner.* The Jesus Prayer is shortened sometimes to "Lord
Jesus Christ, Son of God, have mercy on me." Its shortest form is
"Lord, have mercy."

Our sisters and brothers in the Eastern tradition often use a
prayer rope as they say or sing this simple prayer. The knotted
rope is either wrapped around their wrist or kept in their pocket
to remind them to pray this many times throughout the day—a
constant acknowledgment of their need for the mercy of God.

You may find it helpful to inhale as you say, "Lord Jesus Christ,
Son of God," and then exhale as you petition, "have mercy on me,
a sinner." This rhythm and act of worship helps reset your heart,
mind, body, and spirit.

You also may find it helpful to sing or chant this prayer. Feel
free to make up your own melody or use the tune provided. I
frequently use an Orthodox choir recording. See the Resources
chapter for suggestions.

Confession of Sin

Daily confession has become an essential part of my spiritual
development. It helps me be aware of how I really live. By con-
fessing every day, I keep a short account with myself, God, and
others. It helps prevent me from barreling through life, ignoring
all the warning signs.

As I prepare myself to pray the formal confession, I often ask
myself questions. The questions address sins of both commission
(things I have done) and omission (things I have failed to do).

Have I put off doing what I sensed the Spirit urging me to do? Have I intentionally wronged my sisters and brothers? Have I brought harm unintentionally? Have I spoken harshly or with pride? Have I failed to speak up, merely because it was inconvenient, when I could have defended the righteous cause of another? Have I been so absorbed in myself that I failed to even notice others, much less speak life-giving words to them? Have I looked with envy or covetousness on anyone's life, possessions, or relationships? How have I failed to give God all of me?

As you prepare to pray the confession, be honest with yourself. You know the areas of your own life that look the least like Jesus. You know the areas that consistently fall short of who you know you are created to be. Ask him to reveal areas in which you may be blind to your own sin. Confess, repent, and receive forgiveness. Daily.

The Confession in *The Book of Common Prayer* is written in plural form. When prayed in the context of corporate worship, it is a powerful reminder that we all sin and fall short of the glory of God.[11] I have included the plural form and a more personal, singular form. Alternate between them as you see fit.

Be assured, the One to whom you confess your sins is faithful and forgives *all* your sins. You are "justified by his grace as a gift, through the redemption that is in Christ Jesus."[12]

Psalm 103

Having confessed your sin, return to praise again. This hymn of praise and thanksgiving enumerates the ways in which God has heard and answered the writer's prayers. It serves as a reminder that God is concerned about every detail of your life. The same God who forgives your sin is a healer and redeemer. He is compassionate. He loves you and extends mercy to you. He is worthy of praise! Check the Resources chapter for music options.

Joy Hilley

Prayer for Deliverance and Mercy

This prayer focuses on being set free from those things that tend to plague us again and again. The regular praying of these words helps me be aware of how desperately I need the Spirit to redeem me from these particular snares and to protect me from the Enemy of my soul who delights in my downfall.

I especially love the slightly archaic word *vainglory*, which *Oxford English Dictionary* defines as "Glory that is vain, empty, or worthless; inordinate or unwarranted pride in one's accomplishments or qualities; disposition or tendency to exalt oneself unduly; idle boasting or vaunting."[13] Glory belongs to God, not to you or to me. Good Lord, deliver us.

Psalm 23

Of all the psalms, this may be the most often quoted—and for good reason. The poetic language is exquisite. The writer creates a word picture that brings immediate calm. The opening verses tell me that the Good Shepherd is present. Because he is with me, I do not need to be afraid. I am safe with this shepherd who leads me to meadows with abundant grass and riverbanks with water still enough for me to drink and be refreshed.

I memorized Psalm 23 as a child from a version of the Bible that translated the beginning of the third verse as "He restoreth my soul." Hebrew scholar Robert Alter translates verse 3a as "My life He brings back."[14] He notes that the word often translated as "soul" is more accurately "life breath" and is an image of "someone who has almost stopped breathing and is revived, brought back to life."[15] This good shepherd—who is the same Creator who filled us with his breath—now breathes new life into us. He renews and restores us in *every* way.

As you read this psalm, allow the pastoral images to wash over you. When the metaphor shifts, imagine a table full of good things to eat and an overflowing cup of wine. Then visualize hair that has been luxuriously rubbed with moisturizing oil, knowing that the shepherd cares for your every personal need. Finally, rest in the promise that the shepherd will be with you to the end.

Often, instead of reading this psalm, I listen to it set to music. That way, the melody and words stay with me throughout the day. I've included some of my favorite music settings of Psalm 23 in the Resources chapter.

Psalm or Proverb Reading

Part of being well formed spiritually is being familiar with the scriptures. The psalms are such a rich treasure! They offer a full range of circumstances, emotions, responses to and from God, purposes, and plans. We discover a worldview that is greater than our own. They tell the stories of beauty, hardship, victory, defeat, and every other emotion and event we can imagine!

Feeling discouraged? There's a psalm for that. Feeling hopeful? There's a psalm for that. Ready to burst into a song of praise? Wanting to break the teeth of your enemy or inflict some other form of revenge? Feeling grateful and ready to express thanksgiving? There are psalms for all these situations—and more!

The psalms remind us that no part of human existence is off-limits in our conversation with God. We don't have to pretend to have it all together when we talk with him. The psalms give us permission to be outrageously in love with the Lover of our soul and to ask hard questions about our existence. They allow us to lament, weep, laugh, and rejoice. They provide a fuller understanding of who God is—and how he works throughout human history to redeem and restore all.

The psalms are so important to developing an understanding of God's nature and character—as well as the human condition— that you'll get to read all of them twice each year if you follow the lists[16] provided in the Daily Readings chapter. I encourage you to read the psalms from one translation the first time you go through them and then from a different translation the second time you read the set in a year. The Resources chapter has a brief discussion of translation and paraphrase versions of the Bible.

In between the two sets of psalms, I've included readings from Proverbs. Robert Alter describes the book as an anthology of "admonitions and observations."[17] The poetic language includes satire, humor, pithy remarks, and allegory as it offers advice for moral order, virtue, and wisdom.

If you ever have an opportunity to read Proverbs from Alter's translation, I encourage you to do that. The language is rich, and the commentary is helpful. For the sake of maintaining the flow of your prayer routine, however, I encourage you to wait to read his commentary until you have completed all of the prayers for the day. If you're like me, you might get pulled away into the nuances of language and fail to think of the readings as part of the whole prayer experience.

Gospel Reading

We who call ourselves *Christian* must know the Christ who is fully God and fully man. By reading the accounts of his life, death, resurrection, and ascension, we can't help but fall more deeply in love with him. Using the scripture reading plan of this book, found in Daily Readings chapter, you will read through the Gospels of Matthew, Mark, Luke, and John in the span of a year.

When you read the Gospels, you'll notice that the accounts of Jesus's life and ministry vary somewhat from writer to writer. That is to be expected. For example, if you and I were at an event together, I'm quite sure our descriptions of the evening would differ. You might be prone to pay particular attention to the food or the band. I might be part of a conversation on the other side of the room, which means you probably won't hear any of it. In the same way, each of these Gospel accounts has a unique point of view—a slightly different way of telling the stories of Jesus. Rather than being troubled by these differences, I see them as enriching our understanding of the Son of God and the Son of Man.

Matthew starts with the genealogy of Jesus; highlights Jesus as "teacher"; and concludes with Jesus commissioning the disciples to go, teach, make disciples, and baptize. New Testament scholar N. T. Wright describes the Gospel of Matthew as "trying to bind together the Jewish past and the gentile future."[18] This is the story of Emmanuel, God with us. With us in the manger, in the temple, on the roadside, at the bedside of one who's ill, and in the homes of saints and sinners. The story includes you and me because each of us is commissioned to go and tell the good news. Emmanuel, God with us—forever. Good news, indeed!

In Mark's Gospel, Jesus is identified as the Messiah, the Son of God. The voice of God proclaims his identity, demons declare his identity, and a Roman centurion confirms his identity. While this Gospel bears resemblance to a biography, it reads more like a thriller. Wright describes it as "a story of prophecy and power, resistance and betrayal."[19] What Israel had anticipated and dreamed of in a king and kingdom looked nothing like what they got in the Christ. His power is not used to command armies, but winds and waves. His command brings order and healing; it exorcises evil. Those displays of his divinity are then contrasted with the deep suffering he endures as the Son of Man. The vulnerability of being human brings pain. Ultimately, however, Mark helps the reader understand that Jesus is the Servant-King who has come to usher in a new kingdom. This new kingdom crosses ethnic and social boundaries, extends compassion to the poor and destitute, endures under persecution, and calls disciples to be persistent in prayer.[20]

If Mark is the action-packed telling of the life of Christ, Luke is the kinder, gentler, more inclusive narrative. Luke offers materials not found in any of the other accounts of Jesus. Because of Luke, we have the glorious *Magnificat* and the story of the two disciples on the road to Emmaus. Numerous parables are unique to the third Gospel. Women are given special honor and recognition in his writings. The poor, the marginalized, and the outcast are never overlooked. Luke places an emphasis on the Holy Spirit, whom he details more fully in Acts. The message of salvation is central to this Gospel. And salvation is not limited to the forgiveness of sins. Instead, it includes "deliverance from disaster, healing from physical afflictions, the removal of shame, status reversal ... as well as receiving life, peace, mercy, and grace."[21] Salvation, full and free.

The Gospel of John is rich and deep. For me, reading it is like looking at the facets of a diamond. Fire and brilliance. With each turn, there is more to see. John tells of God's great love and that we need only believe. He recalls how Jesus describes himself: *I am*. He echoes Genesis, Exodus, and Ezekiel with images of a new creation, freedom for all, and living temples where God himself dwells. The language is lavish and lush. Then comes the crushing moment when we see ourselves as Peter—declaring our absolute fidelity only to fall prey to disloyalty. That's when the Good Shepherd, the Lamb of God, the Way, the Truth, the Life, the True Vine, the Resurrection, and the Life takes us aside and asks: *Do you love me?*[22] Then he offers the invitation to us once again: *Follow me.*[23]

Nicene Creed

The Latin word *credo* means "I believe." Christian creeds, therefore, are basic statements of our belief in God. In his letter to the Romans, the Apostle Paul offered an explanation of what constitutes a confession of faith: "If you confess with your lips that Jesus is Lord and believe in your heart that God raised him from the dead, you will be saved."[24]

On the day of Pentecost, when the Holy Spirit fell on the believers and Peter preached to the crowd that assembled, more than three thousand people were converted. They professed that "Jesus is Lord." What had been a small group of believers instantly became a large group and then grew rapidly throughout the world.

Some tenets of the faith and how it should be practiced were clear. Other parts generated questions with which the early church leaders had to wrestle—especially as Gentiles, who did not share a foundation of Judaism, were converted. The spread of Christianity couldn't stop and wait for all the answers. As a result, erroneous teachings—some even rising to the level of heresy—soon followed.

Church leaders then gathered at various times and in various places to debate and determine what beliefs were essential to the Christian faith. In AD 325, they gathered in Nicea (this city of ancient Greece is now in Iznik, Turkey) to address one issue in particular: the co-divinity of Jesus the Son with God the Father. From that council, the Nicene Creed was developed.

In AD 381, the council met at Constantinople (then the capital of the Roman Empire and now Istanbul, Turkey), where they debated once again. Several portions of the Nicene Creed were modified or expanded. Among those changes was the inclusion of Pontius Pilate's name, thereby giving Jesus's life, death, and resurrection a historical context. They also more clearly defined the Spirit's role in relation to the Father and the Son.

By adding "We believe in one holy catholic and apostolic Church," they addressed four essential elements: the Church as *one* (hence the capital *C* as opposed to the lowercase *c* that refers to a particular congregation) emphasizes unity and what we have in common through Christ; the Church as *holy* is set apart from the world for Christian witness; the Church as *catholic* is whole and complete and available to all, regardless of gender, race, ethnicity, or social status (the lowercase *c* is used for *catholic* because it is an adjective, not a title as it would be in the name *Roman Catholic Church*); and the Church as *apostolic* continues the traditions and teachings of Jesus's apostles and is handed down from generation to generation in succession.

Preparatory Verses

These verses remind us that God is far greater than we can comprehend, yet he is absolutely besotted with us and wants to hear from us. Let the truth of these verses settle deep into your heart, to your very core. Allow them to shape what you say as you intercede for yourself and others before the God of the universe. Nothing is off-limits.

Petitions and Intercession for Self, Family, Others

The Apostle Paul calls on us to engage in petitionary prayer, "In everything by prayer and supplication with thanksgiving let your requests be made known to God."[25]

C. S. Lewis reminds us that petitionary prayer is both "allowed and commanded" to us, citing "Give us our daily bread" as an example.[26] He then describes how God invites us to participate in his will through prayer and action: "He seems to do nothing of Himself which He can possibly delegate to His creatures. He commands us to do slowly and blunderingly what He could do perfectly and in the twinkling of an eye."[27]

By this point in the Daily Prayer, you have praised God. You have expressed your adoration of him and joined your voice with angels, archangels, and all the company of heaven. You have confessed your sins before him and received his forgiveness and mercy. You have declared your beliefs. And now—*now*, you can pour out your heart to the Lord!

By waiting to intercede and petition until you have turned your heart and mind toward him, your perspective is properly formed. No longer can you perceive God as some faraway and oblivious god, indifferent to human suffering. He is Emmanuel, God *with* you. He is the One who has redeemed your life from the Pit. He is the Spirit who empowers you to do mighty, holy things and comes alongside you as your comforter and guide. *That's* the God to whom you are praying.

You'll notice that I have arranged each petition and intercession segment on a page by itself. That provides room to write your prayer lists in this book for easy, daily reference. I write my lists on sticky notes and place the notes on the corresponding pages. Not only is this a practical and helpful way to add and delete items from the lists, it also means I can use these pages forever.

As I mentioned in the introduction, I keep a prayer journal. I detail what's on my heart, knowing that the writings are for my eyes only. When prayers are answered, I note that in the journal. I am careful to include the date because the Enemy of my soul inevitably whispers ridiculous lies in my ear. I then can retrieve the journal and point to the day when God heard and answered my cries. This practice has helped my faith grow significantly.

Over the years, I have tried to develop the discipline to agree to pray for someone else only if I'm actually going to do it. Whether I pray for them is determined by the Spirit, as is the duration of my prayers if I'm led to pray for them. When someone asks me to pray, I quickly ask the Spirit if I'm supposed to pray for that person or situation. Sometimes, I sense that I should pray right then and there with whoever is asking. If it comes as a text or an e-mail, I may only respond with "Lord, in your mercy." That is not a slough-off answer. It is a sincere response of "I can do nothing but ask the One who can do it all." Other times, I text or e-mail a longer, more specific prayer. And then, if the Lord leads me,

I add the person or situation to my sticky note lists, where they remain until I am released by the Spirit. I have learned that *not every problem or situation is mine to bear.*

Ask the Spirit to reveal with whom and for what you should partner in prayer. A friend may ask you to pray about her physical or emotional symptom, but the Spirit wants you to pray for the root cause. You won't know that unless you ask the Spirit. A word of caution: unless the Spirit leads otherwise, don't take on additional responsibilities related to the person or situation. Keep your eyes focused on Jesus and the cross. You are not the source of redemption; he is. Pray that his great power and love will come to bear on those situations, events, groups, or individuals. Continue to pray for them each day until he tells you otherwise. Until he releases you from your post, stand firm with your face set like flint toward him.

You may find that your intercessory prayers don't originate from your own needs and observations or from another person requesting prayer. The Spirit frequently calls on us to pray for others. As with all prayer, we are being entrusted with an opportunity to effect change in the spirit realm as well as on earth. Don't jump in and start flailing around in prayer—binding, loosing, and rebuking. Ask the Spirit how to pray and what aspect of the situation is yours to engage in battle.

In addition to praying for individuals, the Spirit calls on us to pray for ministries, those in captivity (both physical and spiritual), nations, institutions, political leaders, strongholds, principalities of darkness, and a host of other things. A word of advice: only take on the subjects and topics he gives you. You always have the power of the Spirit within you; however, you also need his authority to engage.

If someone's name suddenly comes to mind, particularly if you've not thought about or had recent interaction with her, it may be the Spirit prompting you. Ask the Spirit and respond accord-ingly. One night I was awakened—the bolt-up-in-bed kind of awakened—with a man's name in my thoughts. I hadn't seen him in at least fifteen years. I knew I was to pray for him immediately, and I did so for about thirty minutes. I thought of him a few more times in the next several days and prayed briefly. Then nothing. I was released. About two years later, I saw him at a funeral. As we chatted, I realized that he was suicidal the very night I prayed. I never mentioned that I prayed for him, but I knew that God had intervened on his behalf as I interceded for him. Powerful and sobering! Could God have intervened without my prayers? Absolutely. But by including me in the process, he taught me an important lesson—he is actively working on our behalf and some-times asks others to become involved. I am confident that I have been the recipient of unsolicited intercessory prayers as well, and I am eternally grateful for that!

As you bring your petitions to the Lord, you may feel helpless in expressing the depths of what you are sensing or experiencing. You do not have to form the necessary words on your own. The Apostle Paul reminds us, "Likewise the Spirit helps us in our weakness; for we do not know how to pray as we ought, but that very Spirit intercedes with sighs too deep for words. And God, who searches the heart, knows what is the mind of the Spirit, because the Spirit intercedes for the saints according to the will of God."[28] Allow him to groan and intercede for you.

Prayer for Devotion

In between praying for yourself and praying for your family, call on the Lord to once again draw you to himself. Yield your mind, imagination, and will to him—for his glory and for the benefit of others. If the burdens of others are too great to articulate, allow the Spirit to lead you into the deep places for them.

Prayer for Mission and Purpose

I love the imagery of this prayer, especially that of Jesus stretching out his arms of love so that all might be within the reach of his saving embrace. It is prayed immediately before you intercede on behalf of others, as a reminder that every single person is created in the image of God and is loved by him. That perspective is particularly helpful when you are praying about hard situations and people who are difficult to love. Visualize them, then imagine them being within the reach of his saving embrace.

The Lord's Prayer

This prayer unites all Christians everywhere. Distinctions between Roman Catholic, Anglican, Pentecostal, Methodist, Lutheran, Baptist, Eastern Orthodox, Coptic Orthodox, and all other Christian churches fade as soon as the words "Our Father" escape our lips.

As you pray the Lord's Prayer, savor every word. It is succinct and efficient. Every word matters. Do not rush.

You may find it helpful to occasionally sing or listen to a recording of the Lord's Prayer. Several options are included in the Resources chapter.

Contemplation—Sitting With Jesus

By the time you reach this section of the Daily Prayer, you will have read and spoken many words in the previous twenty minutes. It is now time to listen. Be attentive. Wait for him to speak.

Learning to sit with Jesus takes time. It is a discipline, and you *can* learn to do it. If you find your mind wandering to other things, simply refocus yourself and say the name of Jesus. If other thoughts persist, quickly note a couple of words as a reminder, then refocus on Jesus. Be gentle with yourself as you learn to be contemplative.

As a visual person, I find having sacred images around me helps me focus better. One of my favorite objects is a Sacred Heart of Jesus statue. I can see it from where I sit for my prayer time, and looking at it helps get me refocused when my mind wanders. I also have icons of Jesus, crucifixes, crosses, and prayer beads nearby. No, I'm not worshiping idols. I'm using both sides of my brain—the analytical, quantitative side as well as the creative, qualitative side—as I seek the Eternal One who is worthy of all my worship and praise. The visual symbols help guide my thoughts toward him. It's the same as looking at a stained glass window or cross during a church service. They point us back to God.

New Commandments

After sitting with Jesus and listening for his voice, I love reading what he values most—loving him and loving others. I am grateful for the daily reminder to abide, to remain present with him. It resets my heart, mind, soul, and spirit.

Prayer for Peace

The commandments of Jesus compel us to go beyond ourselves and our circles of influence to the world that so desperately needs him. Paul describes the work of Christ Jesus as being our peace, breaking down the dividing wall, providing access to the life-giving presence and power of the Holy Spirit, and making us the dwelling place of God.[29] Hallelujah!

Breastplate of St. Patrick

The mental picture of being surrounded by Jesus—in every direction—is so powerful! When I have a challenging conversation, I recall these words and imagine the cross of Christ between me and the other person. That gives me a healthy degree of separation from their emotions and behaviors.

Joy Hilley

Prayer for Protection

Whether we readily acknowledge it or not, we who follow Christ are opposed by the Enemy of our soul. Sometimes the assaults are big, bold, and obvious. Other times the attacks are subtle and take more time to notice. We must be alert and equipped so we are not caught off guard. As you pray this prayer, imagine yourself putting on each piece of the armor of God—covering yourself from head to toe before picking up the sword and shield—and then choose to pray at all times.

Prayer for Strength and Power in the Spirit

I love the prayer Paul inserts in the middle of his epistle to the Ephesians! As I read it, I visualize the movement of the Spirit deep within me.

Imagine it for yourself. The Holy Spirit moves from the core of your inner being (where your spirit figuratively resides) to your heart (the center of your emotions) to your head (the site of your ability to think and reason). The purpose for this movement? So that you may know in every part of your being the breadth and length and height and depth of God's love, mercy, and grace. That, my friends, is worth a shout of praise!

Prayer of Thanksgiving

As the Daily Prayer draws near its end, I once again give thanks to God for his immeasurable love, the means of grace, and the hope of glory. And I again ask for an awareness of his presence in every circumstance and situation.

Kyrie

Using both the English and Greek, this prayer simply says "Lord, have mercy. Christ, have mercy. Lord, have mercy." The Canaanite woman who displayed great faith as she knelt before Jesus cried out with this plea before she asked that her demon-possessed daughter be healed. So many times, "*Kyrie, eléison*" is the only prayer we have the strength to pray.

Multiple versions of the *Kyrie*—in chant and in song—are referenced in the Resources chapter.

Jesus Prayer

As we conclude our Daily Prayer, we return to the ancient prayer: *Lord Jesus Christ, Son of God, have mercy on me, a sinner.*

Practical Questions Answered

Now that you know the *whys* of the Daily Prayer, you may have some practical *hows* about incorporating it into your life.

When should I pray the Daily Prayer?

For me, the most effective time is in the morning. It orders my heart, mind, and soul for the rest of the day. However, I am keenly aware that you may have young children at home, work nights, or have other commitments that require your attention at the beginning of the day. That's why I intentionally call it *Daily Prayer* not *Morning Prayer.*

Whatever time you select, I encourage you to be as consistent with it as possible. Add it to your calendar reminders and be willing to say you have an appointment at that time. I promise it will become the most important appointment of your day.

Where should I pray the Daily Prayer?

You need to be undisturbed for about thirty minutes to pray through the Daily Prayer. You may not have the luxury of having a separate room where you can go for prayer. If that means sitting alone in your closet, go there. If it means you sit on the staircase, sit there. If you have to sit in an open area with others, then I encourage you to use ear plugs or noise-canceling headphones. Unless you are responsible for the care of someone else who might need urgent assistance, unplug from devices that will distract you.

If at all possible, establish a sacred space in your home. In our current home, it's a corner of a room that is open to other living areas. Since I don't have a way to close off the area, I've selected a time of day that gives me the most privacy. There, I have a comfortable chair, this prayer book, my Bible, a journal, a candle, and headphones. I add the elements to celebrate the Eucharist on a daily basis. Because I can be so easily distracted by notifications on my phone or by the urge to search for more details on a topic, I choose to be analog for everything except music. My music is in a separate file in a streaming app, ready to go. If I come to a word or concept I want to research further, I write it on a list for later. These preparations help me be fully present.

What do I need besides this book?
    Bible

What else might be helpful?
    Journal and writing instrument
    Music
    Cross or crucifix
    Prayer beads or prayer rope
    Icons
    Candles

1   Matthew 6:10
2   Abraham Joshua Heschel, Susannah Heschel, editor, "On Prayer" in *Moral Grandeur and Spiritual Audacity: Essays* (New York: Farrar, Straus and Giroux, 1996), page 258
3   Matthew 6:7
4   Matthew 6:8
5   Matthew 6:9–13
6   Acts 2:42
7   1 Corinthians 10:13
8   The Episcopal Church, *The Book of Common Prayer* (New York, Oxford University Press, 2007), page 361
9   Heschel and Heschel, page 263
10   Heschel and Heschel, page 263
11   Romans 3:23
12   Romans 3:24
13   "vainglory, n." *Oxford English Dictionary Online*. June 2020. Oxford University Press. https://www.oed.com/view/Entry/221089?rskey=2oJk5F&result=1 (accessed June 18, 2020)
14   Robert Alter, *The Book of Psalms: A Translation with Commentary* (New York: W. W. Norton & Company, Inc., 2007), page 78
15   Alter, *The Book of Psalms*, page 78
16   Please note: Psalm 23 is part of the liturgy every day and is, therefore, only included on the Daily Reading lists on February 29 (leap year).
17   Robert Alter, *The Hebrew Bible: Volume 3, The Writings* (New York: W. W. Norton & Company, Inc., 2019), page 342
18   N. T. Wright and Michael F. Bird, *The New Testament In Its World* (Grand Rapids: Zondervan Academic, 2019), page 580
19   Wright and Bird, *The New Testament In Its World*, page 554
20   Wright and Bird, *The New Testament In Its World*, page 577
21   Wright and Bird, *The New Testament In Its World*, page 605
22   John 21:15
23   John 21:19
24   Romans 10:9
25   Philippians 4:6
26   C. S. Lewis, "The Efficacy of Prayer," in *The World's Last Night and Other Essays* (San Francisco: HarperOne, 2017), page 7
27   C. S. Lewis, "The Efficacy of Prayer," page 8
28   Romans 8:26–27
29   Ephesians 2:12–22

Daily Prayer

To him who by the power at work within us
is able to accomplish abundantly far more
than all we can ask or imagine,
to him be glory in the church and in Christ Jesus
to all generations, forever and ever. Amen.

Ephesians 3:20–21

Adoration and Praise

Holy, Holy, Holy Lord, God of power and might,
heaven and earth are full of your glory.
    Hosanna in the highest.
Blessed is he who comes in the name of the Lord.
    Hosanna in the highest.

You are worthy, our Lord and God,
    to receive glory and honor and power,
For you created all things,
    and by your will they existed and were created.

Give thanks to the Lord of Hosts,
    for the Lord is good,
    for his steadfast love endures forever!

Open my lips, O Lord,
    and my mouth shall proclaim your praise.
Create in me a clean heart, O God,
    and renew a right spirit within me.
Cast me not from your presence
    and take not your Holy Spirit from me.
Give me the joy of your saving help again
    and sustain me with your bountiful Spirit.

Glory to the Father, and to the Son, and to the Holy Spirit;
    As it was in the beginning, is now, and will be for ever. Amen.
    [Alleluia!][1]

{During the season of Lent, the Alleluia is omitted.}

Jesus Prayer

Lord Jesus Christ, Son of God,
Have mercy on me, a sinner.

Lord Je- sus Christ, Son   of — God,   have mer-cy   on— me,   a sin - ner.

Confess your sins before continuing.

Confession of Sin

Most merciful God,
    we confess that we have sinned against you
    in thought, word, and deed,
    by what we have done,
    and by what we have left undone.
We have not loved you with our whole heart;
    we have not loved our neighbors as ourselves.
We are truly sorry and we humbly repent.
For the sake of your Son Jesus Christ,
    have mercy on us and forgive us;
    that we may delight in your will,
    and walk in your ways,
    to the glory of your Name. Amen.

—or in the personal form—

Most merciful God,
    I confess that I have sinned against you
    in thought, word, and deed,
    by what I have done,
    and by what I have left undone.
I have not loved you with my whole heart;
    I have not loved my neighbors as myself.
I am truly sorry and I humbly repent.
For the sake of your Son Jesus Christ,
    have mercy on me and forgive me;
    that I may delight in your will,
    and walk in your ways,
    to the glory of your Name. Amen.

Psalm 103

Bless the Lord, O my soul,
    and all that is within me, bless his holy name.
Bless the Lord, O my soul,
    and do not forget all his benefits—
who forgives all your iniquity,
    who heals all your diseases,
who redeems your life from the Pit,
    who crowns you with steadfast love and mercy,
who satisfies you with good as long as you live
    so that your youth is renewed like the eagle's.[2]

Joy Hilley

Prayer for Deliverance and Mercy

From all blindness of heart; from pride, vainglory,
    and hypocrisy; from envy, hatred, and malice;
    and from all want of charity,
Good Lord, deliver me.

From all inordinate and sinful affections;
    and from all the deceits of the world,
    the flesh, and the devil,
Good Lord, deliver me.

From hardness of heart and weariness in well-doing,
Good Lord, deliver me.

God the Father, Creator of heaven and earth,
    God the Son, Redeemer of the world,
    God the Holy Ghost, Sanctifier of the faithful,
Have mercy on me. Amen.

Psalm 23

The Lord is my shepherd, I shall not want.
  He makes me lie down in green pastures;
he leads me beside still waters;
  he restores my soul.
He leads me in right paths for his name's sake.
Even though I walk through the darkest valley,
  I fear no evil;
for you are with me;
  your rod and your staff—they comfort me.
You prepare a table before me
  in the presence of my enemies;
you anoint my head with oil; my cup overflows.
Surely goodness and mercy shall follow me
  all the days of my life,
and I shall dwell in the house of the Lord
  my whole life long.[3]

Psalm or Proverb Reading

The Daily Readings lists are in the next chapter.

Gospel Reading

The Daily Readings lists are in the next chapter.

Nicene Creed

We believe in one God,
 the Father, the Almighty,
 maker of heaven and earth,
 of all that is, seen and unseen.

We believe in one Lord, Jesus Christ,
 the only Son of God,
 eternally begotten of the Father,
God from God, Light from Light,
 true God from true God,
 begotten, not made,
 of one Being with the Father.
Through him all things were made.
For us and for our salvation
 he came down from heaven:
by the power of the Holy Spirit
 he became incarnate from the Virgin Mary,
 and was made man.
For our sake he was crucified under Pontius Pilate;
 he suffered death and was buried.

Joy Hilley

On the third day he rose again
in accordance with the Scriptures;
he ascended into heaven
and is seated at the right hand of the Father.
He will come again in glory to judge the living and the
dead, and his kingdom will have no end.

We believe in the Holy Spirit, the Lord, the giver of life,
who proceeds from the Father and the Son.
With the Father and the Son he is worshiped
and glorified.
He has spoken through the Prophets.

We believe in one holy catholic and apostolic Church.
We acknowledge one baptism for the forgiveness of sins.
We look for the resurrection of the dead,
and the life of the world to come. Amen.

Preparatory Verses

I am the Lord, the God of all flesh;
    is anything too hard for me?[4]

Call to me and I will answer you,
    and will tell you great and hidden things
    that you have not known.[5]

The steadfast love of the Lord never ceases,
    his mercies never come to an end;
they are new every morning;
    great is your faithfulness.
"The Lord is my portion," says my soul,
    "therefore I will hope in him."[6]

Petitions and Intercession for Self

Prayer for Devotion

Almighty and eternal God,
    draw our hearts to you.
So guide our minds,
    so fill our imaginations,
    so control our wills,
    that we may be wholly yours,
    utterly dedicated to you.
Use us then, we pray, as you will,
    always to your glory
    and for the welfare of your people;
    through our Lord and Savior Jesus Christ. Amen.

Petitions and Intercession for Family

Prayer for Mission and Purpose

Lord Jesus Christ, you stretched out your arms of love upon the
hard wood of the cross that everyone might come within the
reach of your saving embrace:

So clothe us in your Spirit that we, reaching forth our hands in
love, may bring those who do not know you to the knowledge
and love of you;

For the honor of your Name. Amen.

Petitions and Intercession for Others

The Lord's Prayer

Our Father, who art in heaven,
   hallowed be thy Name,
   thy kingdom come,
   thy will be done,
      on earth as it is in heaven.
Give us this day our daily bread.
And forgive us our trespasses,
   as we forgive those
   who trespass against us.
And lead us not into temptation,
   but deliver us from evil.
For thine is the kingdom,
   and the power, and the glory,
   for ever and ever. Amen.

Joy Hilley

Contemplation—Sitting With Jesus

New Commandments

I give you a new commandment, that you love one another. Just as I have loved you, you also should love one another. By this everyone will know that you are my disciples, if you have love for one another.[7]

Abide in me as I abide in you. Just as the branch cannot bear fruit by itself unless it abides in the vine, neither can you unless you abide in me. I am the vine, you are the branches. Those who abide in me and I in them bear much fruit, because apart from me you can do nothing.[8]

"You shall love the Lord your God with all your heart, and with all your soul, and with all your mind." This is the greatest and first commandment. And a second is like it: "You shall love your neighbor as yourself." On these two commandments hang all the law and the prophets.[9]

Prayer for Peace

O God, you have made of one blood
    all the peoples of the earth,
    and sent your blessed Son
    to preach peace to those who are far off
    and to those who are near.
Grant that people everywhere
    may seek after you and find you.
Bring the nations into your fold.
Pour out your Spirit upon all flesh.
And hasten the coming of your kingdom;
    through Jesus Christ our Lord. Amen.

Breastplate of St. Patrick

Christ with me, Christ before me,
Christ behind me, Christ within me,
Christ beneath me, Christ above me,
Christ at my right, Christ at my left,
Christ when I lie down,
Christ when I sit down,
Christ when I arise,
Christ in the heart of everyone who thinks of me,
Christ in the mouth of everyone who speaks of me,
Christ in every eye that sees me,
Christ in every ear that hears me.[10]

Prayer for Protection

Lord Jesus, I now put on the whole armor of God,
　　so that I may be able to stand firm
　　against the wiles of the devil.
I clothe myself with the helmet of salvation and
　　the breastplate of righteousness.
I fasten the belt of truth around my waist.
As shoes for my feet, I put on whatever will make me
　　ready to proclaim the gospel of peace.
I take up the shield of faith, with which I can quench all the
　　flaming arrows of the evil one, and the sword of the Spirit,
　　which is the word of God.
I choose to pray in the Spirit at all times in every prayer
　　and supplication. I will remain alert and will persevere
　　in praying for all God's people.
In the name of the Father, the Son, and the Holy Ghost. Amen.[11]

Prayer for Strength and Power in the Spirit

Almighty God, I bow my knees before the Father,
    from whom every family in heaven and on earth
    takes its name.
According to the riches of your glory,
    I pray that you will strengthen me in my inner being,
    with power through your Spirit,
        and that Christ will dwell in my heart through faith,
    as I am rooted and grounded in love.
Grant me, O God, the power to comprehend,
    with all the saints,
    what is the breadth and length and height and depth
    of your love, mercy, and grace.
Grant that I may know the love of Christ that surpasses
    knowledge, so that I may be filled with all the
    fullness of God. Amen.[12]

Joy Hilley

Prayer of Thanksgiving

Almighty God, Father of all mercies,
We your unworthy servants give you humble thanks
    for all your goodness and loving kindness to us and
    all whom you have made.
We bless you for our creation, preservation, and
    all the blessings of this life;
But above all for your immeasurable love in the
    redemption of the world by our Lord Jesus Christ,
For the means of grace, and for the hope of glory.
And, we pray, give us such an awareness of your mercies,
    that with truly thankful hearts we may show forth your praise,
    not only with our lips, but in our lives,
        by giving up ourselves to your service,
        and by walking before you
        in holiness and righteousness all our days;
Through Jesus Christ our Lord, to whom,
    with you and the Holy Spirit,
    be honor and glory throughout all ages. Amen.

Kyrie

Lord, have mercy.
Christ, have mercy.
Lord, have mercy.

Kyrie, eléison.
Christe, eléison.
Kyrie, eléison.

Jesus Prayer

Lord Jesus Christ, Son of God,
Have mercy on me, a sinner.

Lord Je- sus Christ, Son of — God, have mer-cy on — me, a sin - ner.

---

1   Includes texts from *The Book of Common Prayer*, Revelation 4:11, Psalm 107, Psalm 51
2   Psalm 103:1–5
3   Psalm 23
4   Jeremiah 32:27
5   Jeremiah 33:3
6   Lamentations 3:22–24
7   John 13:34–35
8   John 15:4–5
9   Matthew 22:37–40
10 Traditionally attributed to Saint Patrick, fifth century
11 Drawn from Ephesians 6:11, 13–18
12 Drawn from Ephesians 3:14–19

Joy Hilley

Daily Readings

The Lord bless you and keep you;
the Lord make his face to shine upon you,
and be gracious to you;
the Lord lift up his countenance upon you,
and give you peace.

Numbers 6:24–26

January Readings

February Readings

February 1 ....Psalm 33 ....Matthew 11:20–30
February 2 ....Psalm 34 ....Matthew 12:1–8
February 3 ....Psalm 35 ....Matthew 12:9–21
February 4 ....Psalm 36 ....Matthew 12:22–32
February 5 ....Psalm 37........................Matthew 12:33–42
February 6 ....Psalm 38 ....Matthew 12:43–50
February 7 ....Psalm 39 ....Matthew 13:1–9
February 8 ....Psalm 40 ....Matthew 13:10–17
February 9 ....Psalm 41 ....Matthew 13:18–30
February 10 ....Psalm 42 ....Matthew 13:31–43
February 11........................Psalm 43 ....Matthew 13:44–53
February 12........................Psalm 44........................Matthew 13:54–58
February 13........................Psalm 45 ....Matthew 14:1–12
February 14 ....Psalm 46........................Matthew 14:13–21
February 15........................Psalm 47 ....Matthew 14:22–33
February 16 ....Psalm 48........................Matthew 14:34–36
February 17........................Psalm 49 ....Matthew 15:1–9
February 18 ....Psalm 50 ....Matthew 15:10–20
February 19 ....Psalm 51 ....Matthew 15:21–28
February 20 ....Psalm 52........................Matthew 15:29–39
February 21........................Psalm 53 ....Matthew 16:1–12
February 22........................Psalm 54 ....Matthew 16:13–20
February 23........................Psalm 55 ....Matthew 16:21–28
February 24 ....Psalm 56 ....Matthew 17:1–13
February 25........................Psalm 57........................Matthew 17:14–21
February 26........................Psalm 58 ....Matthew 17:22–27
February 27 ....Psalm 59 ....Matthew 18:1–9
February 28 ....Psalm 60........................Matthew 18:10–22
February 29........................Psalm 23 ....Romans 4:13–25

Joy Hilley

March Readings

April Readings

May Readings

June Readings

Joy Hilley

July Readings

August Readings

August 1	Psalm 7	Luke 7:18–23
August 2	Psalm 8	Luke 7:24–35
August 3	Psalm 9	Luke 7:36–50
August 4	Psalm 10	Luke 8:1–3
August 5	Psalm 11	Luke 8:4–10
August 6	Psalm 12	Luke 8:11–15
August 7	Psalm 13	Luke 8:16–21
August 8	Psalm 14	Luke 8:22–25
August 9	Psalm 15	Luke 8:26–39
August 10	Psalm 16	Luke 8:40–48
August 11	Psalm 17	Luke 8:49–56
August 12	Psalm 18	Luke 9:1–6
August 13	Psalm 19	Luke 9:7–9
August 14	Psalm 20	Luke 9:10–17
August 15	Psalm 21	Luke 9:18–20
August 16	Psalm 22	Luke 9:21–27
August 17	Psalm 24	Luke 9:28–36
August 18	Psalm 25	Luke 9:37–43a
August 19	Psalm 26	Luke 9:43b–45
August 20	Psalm 27	Luke 9:46—50
August 21	Psalm 28	Luke 9:51–56
August 22	Psalm 29	Luke 9:57–62
August 23	Psalm 30	Luke 10:1–12
August 24	Psalm 31	Luke 10:13–16
August 25	Psalm 32	Luke 10:17–24
August 26	Psalm 33	Luke 10:25–37
August 27	Psalm 34	Luke 10:38–42
August 28	Psalm 35	Luke 11:1–4
August 29	Psalm 36	Luke 11:5–13
August 30	Psalm 37	Luke 11:14–23
August 31	Psalm 38	Luke 11:24–28

Joy Hilley

September Readings

October Readings

November Readings

December Readings

December 1 .... Psalm 120 .... John 11:45–57

December 2 .... Psalm 121 .... John 12:1–11

December 3 .... Psalm 122 .... John 12:12–19

December 4 .... Psalm 123 .... John 12:20–26

December 5 .... Psalm 124 .... John 12:27–36a

December 6 .... Psalm 125 .... John 12:36b–43

December 7 .... Psalm 126 .... John 12:44–50

December 8 .... Psalm 127 .... John 13:1–20

December 9 .... Psalm 128 .... John 13:21–30

December 10 .... Psalm 129 .... John 13:31–38

December 11 .... Psalm 130 .... John 14:1–14

December 12 .... Psalm 131 .... John 14:15–31

December 13 .... Psalm 132 .... John 15:1–17

December 14 .... Psalm 133 .... John 15:18–16:4a

December 15 .... Psalm 134 .... John 16:4b–15

December 16 .... Psalm 135 .... John 16:16–24

December 17 .... Psalm 136 .... John 16:25–33

December 18 .... Psalm 137 .... John 17:1–26

December 19 .... Psalm 138 .... John 18:1–11

December 20 .... Psalm 139 .... John 18:12–18

December 21 .... Psalm 140 .... John 18:19–27

December 22 .... Psalm 141 .... John 18:28–38a

December 23 .... Psalm 142 .... John 18:38b–19:16a

December 24 .... Psalm 143 .... John 19:16b–30

December 25 .... Psalm 144 .... John 19:31–37

December 26 .... Psalm 145 .... John 19:38–42

December 27 .... Psalm 146 .... John 20:1–10

December 28 .... Psalm 147 .... John 20:11–18

December 29 .... Psalm 148 .... John 20:19–31

December 30 .... Psalm 149 .... John 21:1–14

December 31 .... Psalm 150 .... John 21:15–25

Joy Hilley

Daily Eucharist

May our Lord Jesus Christ himself
and God our Father, who loved us and
through grace gave us eternal comfort and good hope,
comfort your hearts and strengthen them
in every good work and word.

II Thessalonians 2:16–17

Taking communion daily has been one of the most holy and transformative experiences of my life. I invite you to consider including it in your daily practice as well.

I realize that taking communion at home—without a priest or pastor to lead or bless the elements—is controversial for Christians from some traditions. If it is problematic for you, based on your church's teachings or your personal convictions, please know that I respect and honor your view. This will have to be a topic on which we agree to disagree! I join with the Apostle Paul in praying that we will exhibit "humility and gentleness, with patience, bearing with one another in love, making every effort to maintain the unity of the Spirit in the bond of peace."[1]

For me, the Eucharist should only be celebrated after having said or sung praise, prayed a form of the Jesus Prayer, read a psalm and the Gospel lesson, recited a creed of faith, and confessed one's sin. Because it is a sacred and holy privilege, I believe it should be observed with dignity and solemnity, as well as great joy. The liturgy in the Daily Prayer chapter prepares your heart, mind, and spirit to receive this blessed sacrament. If you choose to serve yourself holy communion at home, please first participate in the Daily Prayer.

Because I alternate between liturgies for communion, I have included two in this chapter. Ask the Spirit to show you which to use each day.

Holy Eucharist Liturgy 1
To be celebrated after completing the Daily Prayer liturgy

Bless the Lord who forgives all my sins;
　His mercy endures for ever.

Lamb of God, you take away the sins of the world,
　have mercy on me.
Lamb of God, you take away the sins of the world,
　have mercy on me.
Lamb of God, you take away the sins of the world,
　grant your peace.

Lift up your hearts.
Give thanks to the Lord our God.
It is right to give him thanks and praise.

　It is right, and a good and joyful thing, always and everywhere to give thanks to you, Father Almighty, Creator of heaven and earth.

　Therefore we praise you, joining our voices with angels and archangels and with all the company of heaven, who for ever sing this hymn to proclaim the glory of your Name:

> *Holy, Holy, Holy Lord, God of power and might,*
> 　*heaven and earth are full of your glory.*
> *Hosanna in the highest.*
> *Blessed is he who comes in the name of the Lord.*
> *Hosanna in the highest.*

　Holy and gracious Father: In your infinite love you made us for yourself; and, when we had fallen into sin and become subject to evil and death, you, in your mercy, sent Jesus Christ, your only and eternal Son, to share our human nature, to live and die as one of us, to reconcile us to you, the God and Father of all.

He stretched out his arms upon the cross, and offered himself, in obedience to your will, a perfect sacrifice for the whole world.

{At the following words concerning the bread, hold or lay a hand upon it; at the words concerning the cup, hold or place a hand upon the cup of wine.}

On the night he was handed over to suffering and death, our Lord Jesus Christ took bread; and when he had given thanks to you, he broke it, and gave it to his disciples, and said, "Take, eat: This is my Body, which is given for you. Do this for the remembrance of me."

After supper he took the cup of wine; and when he had given thanks, he gave it to them, and said, "Drink this, all of you: This is my Blood of the new Covenant, which is shed for you and for many for the forgiveness of sins. Whenever you drink it, do this for the remembrance of me."

Therefore we proclaim the mystery of faith:

> *Christ has died.*
> *Christ is risen.*
> *Christ will come again.*

We celebrate the memorial of our redemption, O Father, in this sacrifice of praise and thanksgiving. Recalling his death, resurrection, and ascension, we offer you these gifts.

Sanctify them by your Holy Spirit to be for your people the Body and Blood of your Son, the holy food and drink of new and unending life in him. Sanctify us also that we may faithfully receive this holy Sacrament, and serve you in unity, constancy, and peace;

and at the last day bring us with all your saints into the joy of your eternal kingdom.

All this we ask through your Son Jesus Christ. By him, and with him, and in him, in the unity of the Holy Spirit all honor and glory is yours, Almighty Father, now and for ever. Amen.

{During the season of Lent, the following Alleluias are omitted.}

[Alleluia.] Christ our Passover is sacrificed for us;
Therefore let us keep the feast. [Alleluia.]

The Body of Christ, the bread of heaven. Amen.
{Eat the bread.}

The Blood of Christ, the cup of salvation. Amen.
{Drink the wine.}

Eternal God, heavenly Father, you have graciously accepted us as living members of your Son our Savior Jesus Christ, and you have fed us with spiritual food in the Sacrament of his Body and Blood.

Send us now into the world in peace, and grant us strength and courage to love and serve you with gladness and singleness of heart; through Christ our Lord. Amen.

Thanks be to God. Amen.

Holy Eucharist Liturgy 2

To be celebrated after completing the Daily Prayer liturgy

Lord God of our Fathers: God of Abraham, Isaac, and Jacob; God and Father of our Lord Jesus Christ: Open our eyes to see your hand at work in the world about us.

Deliver us from the presumption of coming to this Table for solace only, and not for strength; for pardon only, and not for renewal. Let the grace of this Holy Communion make us one body, one spirit in Christ, that we may worthily serve the world in his name.

Risen Lord, be known to us in the breaking of the Bread.

Accept these prayers and praises, Father, through Jesus Christ our great High Priest, to whom, with you and the Holy Spirit, your Church gives honor, glory, and worship, from generation to generation. Amen.

It is truly right to glorify you, Father, and to give you thanks; for you alone are God, living and true, dwelling in light inaccessible from before time and for ever.

Fountain of life and source of all goodness, you made all things and fill them with your blessing; you created them to rejoice in the splendor of your radiance.

Countless throngs of angels stand before you to serve you night and day; and, beholding the glory of your presence, they offer you unceasing praise. Joining with them, and giving voice to every creature under heaven, we acclaim you, and glorify your Name, as we say,

> *Holy, Holy, Holy Lord, God of power and might,*
> *heaven and earth are full of your glory.*

Hosanna in the highest.
Blessed is he who comes in the name of the Lord.
Hosanna in the highest.

We acclaim you, holy Lord, glorious in power. Your mighty works reveal your wisdom and love.

You formed us in your own image, giving the whole world into our care, so that, in obedience to you, our Creator, we might rule and serve all your creatures.

When our disobedience took us far from you, you did not abandon us to the power of death. In your mercy you came to our help, so that in seeking you we might find you. Again and again you called us into covenant with you, and through the prophets you taught us to hope for salvation.

Father, you loved the world so much that in the fullness of time you sent your only Son to be our Savior. Incarnate by the Holy Spirit, born of the Virgin Mary, he lived as one of us, yet without sin.

To the poor he proclaimed the good news of salvation; to prisoners, freedom; to the sorrowful, joy. To fulfill your purpose he gave himself up to death; and, rising from the grave, destroyed death, and made the whole creation new.

And, that we might live no longer for ourselves, but for him who died and rose for us, he sent the Holy Spirit, his own first gift for those who believe, to complete his work in the world, and to bring to fulfillment the sanctification of all.

Joy Hilley

{At the following words concerning the bread, hold or lay a hand upon it; at the words concerning the cup, hold or place a hand upon the cup of wine.}

When the hour had come for him to be glorified by you, his heavenly Father, having loved his own who were in the world, he loved them to the end; at supper with them he took bread, and when he had given thanks to you, he broke it, and gave it to his disciples, and said, "Take, eat: This is my Body, which is given for you. Do this for the remembrance of me."

After supper he took the cup of wine; and when he had given thanks, he gave it to them, and said, "Drink this, all of you: This is my Blood of the new Covenant, which is shed for you and for many for the forgiveness of sins. Whenever you drink it, do this for the remembrance of me."

Father, we now celebrate this memorial of our redemption. Recalling Christ's death and his descent among the dead, proclaiming his resurrection and ascension to your right hand, awaiting his coming in glory; and offering to you, from the gifts you have given us, this bread and this cup, we praise you and we bless you.

Lord, we pray that in your goodness and mercy your Holy Spirit may descend upon us, and upon these gifts, sanctifying them and showing them to be holy gifts for your holy people, the bread of life and the cup of salvation, the Body and Blood of your Son Jesus Christ.

Grant that all who share this bread and cup may become one body and one spirit, a living sacrifice in Christ, to the praise of your Name.

Remember, Lord, your one holy catholic and apostolic Church, redeemed by the blood of your Christ. Reveal its unity, guard its faith, and preserve it in peace.

Grant that we may find our inheritance with all the saints who have found favor with you in ages past. We praise you in union with them and give you glory through your Son Jesus Christ our Lord.

Through Christ, and with Christ, and in Christ, all honor and glory are yours, Almighty God and Father, in the unity of the Holy Spirit, for ever and ever. Amen.

{During the season of Lent, the following Alleluias are omitted.}

[Alleluia.] Christ our Passover is sacrificed for us;
Therefore let us keep the feast. [Alleluia.]

The Body of Christ, the bread of heaven. Amen.
{Eat the bread.}

The Blood of Christ, the cup of salvation. Amen.
{Drink the wine.}

Eternal God, heavenly Father, you have graciously accepted us as living members of your Son our Savior Jesus Christ, and you have fed us with spiritual food in the Sacrament of his Body and Blood.

Send us now into the world in peace, and grant us strength and courage to love and serve you with gladness and singleness of heart; through Christ our Lord. Amen.

Thanks be to God. Amen.

---

1   Ephesians 4:2–3

Joy Hilley

Supplemental Prayers

Blessed be the God and Father of our Lord Jesus Christ,
who has blessed us in Christ with every spiritual blessing
in the heavenly places. In him we have redemption
through his blood, the forgiveness of our trespasses,
according to the riches of his grace that he lavished on us.

Ephesians 1:3, 7–8a

When I say I've been going to church all my life, it's not just an expression. I attended my first church service at the Marine Corps Base Camp Lejeune chapel, where my father was the chaplain. I was six weeks old. As the daughter of a career navy officer, I experienced a lot of change as we moved from duty station to duty station on both coasts of the States—as well as a post in Morocco. Every couple of years, I adjusted to a new school, a new house in a new neighborhood, new customs, and new friends. The two things that were most familiar in those new places were the services at the base chapel and our piano at home; both formed me.

Depending on how many chaplains were assigned to a particular location and what denominations they represented, I might hear a sermon from a Baptist, Lutheran, Episcopal, or Methodist on any given Sunday. When I became old enough to drive, I began exploring civilian churches on my own. I went with friends to Presbyterian, Nazarene, and Greek Orthodox churches. Even my parents were members of different denominations, so my Christian training was eclectic on all fronts!

By the time I enrolled in seminary, I'd experienced a wide range of worship practices in both high and low church settings. Communion every Sunday. Communion once a quarter. Organ preludes and postludes. Full bands with guitars, drums, keyboard, and strings. Incense. Candles. Spotlights. Stunning stained glass windows. Minimalist clear panes.

As a student in the Christian education *and* church music disciplines, I learned the basics of church history, had an overview of the Old and New Testaments, explored worship, and studied several books of the Bible in depth for my core classes. My major courses trained me to teach and disciple others—all things one would expect at a conservative Christian seminary.

The twist came in my music classes. Yes, I learned to play the piano better, my voice was trained for traditional church music, and I gained experience in choral and orchestral conducting. But one class introduced me to the Latin Mass and Gregorian chant. There, I memorized the major portions of the mass—known as the "ordinary" sections—in Latin and learned to distinguish between the eight modes of the chants merely by hearing the first two notes. While the class was often lighthearted—and occasionally bordered on the ridiculous as we all learned to chant—the seeds of ancient worship were planted deep within my soul. Those classes, combined with my diverse church upbringing, informed my development of the Daily Prayer.

In writing this book, I realized there are other prayers and texts I use on a regular basis, although not daily. Some of these are so beautiful and meaningful that I couldn't resist offering them in this chapter, in no particular order. Not surprisingly, they come from various Christian traditions. May they be a blessing to you!

Te Deum laudamus
a hymn of praise from the third or fourth century

You are God: we praise you;
You are the Lord; we acclaim you;
You are the eternal Father:
All creation worships you.
To you all angels, all the powers of heaven,
Cherubim and Seraphim, sing in endless praise:
    Holy, holy, holy Lord, God of power and might,
    heaven and earth are full of your glory.
The glorious company of apostles praise you.
The noble fellowship of prophets praise you.
The white-robed army of martyrs praise you.
Throughout the world the holy Church acclaims you;
    Father, of majesty unbounded,
        your true and only Son, worthy of all worship,
        and the Holy Spirit, advocate and guide.
You, Christ, are the king of glory,
    the eternal Son of the Father.
When you became man to set us free
    you did not shun the Virgin's womb.
You overcame the sting of death
    and opened the kingdom of heaven to all believers.
You are seated at God's right hand in glory.
We believe that you will come and be our judge.
Come then, Lord, and help your people,
    bought with the price of your own blood,
    and bring us with your saints
    to glory everlasting.

Venite
Psalm 95:1–7

O come, let us sing to the Lord;
    let us make a joyful noise to the rock of our salvation!
Let us come into his presence with thanksgiving;
    let us make a joyful noise to him with songs of praise!
For the Lord is a great God,
    and a great King above all gods.
In his hand are the depths of the earth;
    the heights of the mountains are his also.
The sea is his, for he made it,
    and the dry land, which his hands have formed.
O come, let us worship and bow down,
    let us kneel before the Lord, our Maker!
For he is our God,
    and we are the people of his pasture,
    and the sheep of his hand.
O that today you would listen to his voice!

Joy Hilley

The First Song of Isaiah (Ecce, Deus)
Isaiah 12:2–6

Surely, it is God who saves me;
    I will trust in him and not be afraid.
For the Lord is my stronghold and my sure defense,
    and he will be my Savior.
Therefore you shall draw water with rejoicing
    from the springs of salvation.
And on that day you shall say,
    Give thanks to the Lord and call upon his Name;
Make his deeds known among the peoples;
    see that they remember that his Name is exalted.
Sing the praises of the Lord, for he has done great things,
    and this is known in all the world.
Cry aloud, inhabitants of Zion, ring out your joy,
    for the great one in the midst of you is the Holy One of Israel.

The Second Song of Isaiah (Quaerite Dominum)
Isaiah 55:6–11

Seek the Lord while he wills to be found;
    call upon him when he draws near.
Let the wicked forsake their ways
    and the evil ones their thoughts;
And let them turn to the Lord, and he will have compassion,
    and to our God, for he will richly pardon.
For my thoughts are not your thoughts,
    nor your ways my ways, says the Lord.
For as the heavens are higher than the earth,
    so are my ways higher than your ways,
    and my thoughts than your thoughts.
For as rain and snow fall from the heavens
    and return not again, but water the earth,
Bringing forth life and giving growth,
    seed for sowing and bread for eating,
So is my word that goes forth from my mouth;
    it will not return to me empty;
But it will accomplish that which I have purposed,
    and prosper in that for which I sent it.

Joy Hilley

The Third Song of Isaiah (Surge, illuminare)
Isaiah 60:1–3, 11a, 14c, 18–19

Arise, shine, for your light has come,
    and the glory of the Lord has dawned upon you.
For behold, darkness covers the land;
    deep gloom enshrouds the peoples.
But over you the Lord will rise,
    and his glory will appear upon you.
Nations will stream to your light,
    and kings to the brightness of your dawning.
Your gates will always be open;
    by day or night they will never be shut.
They will call you, The City of the Lord,
    The Zion of the Holy One of Israel.
Violence will no more be heard in your land,
    ruin or destruction within your borders.
You will call your walls, Salvation,
    and all your portals, Praise.
The sun will no more be your light by day;
    by night you will not need the brightness of the moon.
The Lord will be your everlasting light,
    and your God will be your glory.

The Song of Mary (Magnificat)
Luke 1:46–55

My soul proclaims the greatness of the Lord,
    my spirit rejoices in God my Savior;
    for he has looked with favor on his lowly servant.
From this day all generations will call me blessed:
    the Almighty has done great things for me,
    and holy is his Name.
He has mercy on those who fear him
    in every generation.
He has shown the strength of his arm,
    he has scattered the proud in their conceit.
He has cast down the mighty from their thrones,
    and has lifted up the lowly.
He has filled the hungry with good things,
    and the rich he has sent away empty.
He has come to the help of his servant Israel
    for he has remembered his promise of mercy,
    the promise he made to our fathers,
    to Abraham and his children for ever.

A Song to the Lamb (Dignus es)
Revelation 4:11, 5:9–10, 13

Splendor and honor and kingly power
    are yours by right, O Lord our God,
For you created everything that is,
    and by your will they were created and have their being;
And yours by right, O Lamb that was slain,
    for with your blood you have redeemed for God,
From every family, language, people, and nation,
    a kingdom of priests to serve our God.

And so, to him who sits upon the throne,
    and to Christ the Lamb,
Be worship and praise, dominion and splendor,
    for ever and for evermore.

Gloria in Excelsis

Glory to God in the highest,
    and peace to his people on earth.
Lord God, heavenly King,
almighty God and Father,
    we worship you, we give you thanks,
    we praise you for your glory.

Lord Jesus Christ, only Son of the Father,
Lord God, Lamb of God,
you take away the sin of the world:
    have mercy on us;
you are seated at the right hand of the Father:
    receive our prayer.

For you alone are the Holy One,
you alone are the Lord,
you alone are the Most High,
    Jesus Christ,
    with the Holy Spirit,
    in the glory of God the Father. Amen.

Joy Hilley

Evening Prayers

Keep watch, dear Lord, with those who work, or watch, or weep this night, and give your angels charge over those who sleep. Tend the sick, Lord Christ; give rest to the weary, bless the dying, soothe the suffering, pity the afflicted, shield the joyous; and all for your love's sake. Amen.

Be present, O merciful God, and protect us through the hours of this night, so that we who are wearied by the changes and chances of this life may rest in your eternal changelessness; through Jesus Christ our Lord. Amen.

Look down, O Lord, from your heavenly throne, and illumine this night with your celestial brightness; that by night as by day your people may glorify your holy Name; through Jesus Christ our Lord. Amen.

Be our light in the darkness, O Lord, in your great mercy. Defend us from all perils and dangers of this night. Guard us from all snares of the Enemy. Let your holy angels dwell with us to preserve us in peace, and let your blessing be upon us always, for the love of your only Son, our Savior Jesus Christ. Amen.

Solemn Prayers

Almighty God, kindle, we pray, in every heart the true love of peace, and guide with your wisdom those who take counsel for the nations of the earth, that in tranquility your dominion may increase, until the earth is filled with the knowledge of your love; through Jesus Christ our Lord. Amen.

For all who suffer and are afflicted in body or in mind:

> For the hungry and the homeless, the destitute,
>   and the oppressed;
> For the sick, the wounded, and the crippled;
> For those in loneliness, fear, and anguish;
> For those who face temptation, doubt, and despair;
> For the sorrowful and bereaved; and
> For prisoners, captives, and those in mortal danger,

We pray that God in his mercy will comfort and relieve them, and grant them the knowledge of his love, and stir up in us the will and patience to minister to their needs. Amen.

Gracious God, the comfort of all who sorrow, the strength of all who suffer: Let the cry of those in misery and need come to you, that they may find your mercy present with them in all their afflictions; and give us, we pray, the strength to serve them for the sake of him who suffered for us, your Son Jesus Christ our Lord. Amen.

Joy Hilley

Merciful God, Creator of all the peoples of the earth and lover of souls: Have compassion on all who do not know you as you are revealed in your Son Jesus Christ.

For all who have not received the Gospel of Christ:

> For those who have never heard the word of salvation;
> For those who have lost their faith;
> For those hardened by sin or indifference;
> For the contemptuous and the scornful;
> For those who are enemies of the cross of Christ and
>   persecutors of his disciples; and
> For those who in the name of Christ have persecuted others,

Let your Gospel be preached with grace and power to them. Open their hearts to the truth, and lead them to faith and obedience. May there be one flock under one shepherd, Jesus Christ our Lord. Amen.

O God of unchangeable power and eternal light: Look favorably on your whole Church, that wonderful and sacred mystery; by the effectual working of your providence, carry out in tranquility the plan of salvation; let the whole world see and know that things which were cast down are being raised up, and things which had grown old are being made new, and that all things are being brought to their perfection by him through whom all things were made, your Son Jesus Christ our Lord; who lives and reigns with you, in the unity of the Holy Spirit, one God, for ever and ever. Amen.

African Blessing[1]

All our problems,
  We send to the cross of Christ!

All our difficulties,
  We send to the cross of Christ!

All the devil's works,
  We send to the cross of Christ!

All our hopes,
  We set on the risen Christ!

---

1 Graham Kings and Geoff Morgan, *Offerings from Kenya to Anglicanism: Liturgical Texts and Contexts including 'A Kenyan Service of Holy Communion'* (Cambridge: Grove Books Limited, 2001), pages 24–25

This blessing is based on an ancient litany of the nomadic Turkana ethnic group in northern Kenya. Traditionally the Turkana, with a dramatic sweep of their arms to the west, sent all their problems, difficulties, and works of evil to the Karamajong, a nomadic ethnic group in what is now Uganda.

When a group of the Turkana became Christians, the litany changed. What once was intended as a curse on their enemies was transformed into a blessing.

Now, throughout Anglican churches in Africa, worship services often end with this blessing. Using the same dramatic sweep of their arms, congregants send all their problems, difficulties, and the devil's works to the cross. And with hands raised, they set their hopes on the risen Christ.

In the early 2000s (the exact date is a blur because we had a new baby in our house), I had the opportunity to be in a worship service led by the Most Reverend Henry Orombi, Archbishop of the Church of Uganda. As I knelt at the altar rail, he placed his hands on my head and prayed a blessing on me. A sacred and holy moment. That congregation used this blessing at the conclusion of their service, complete with the hand motions. I encourage you to try it. Be dramatic!

Joy Hilley

Resources

*We have not ceased praying for you and asking that you
may be filled with the knowledge of God's will in all
spiritual wisdom and understanding, so that you may
lead lives worthy of the Lord, fully pleasing to him,
as you bear fruit in every good work and
as you grow in the knowledge of God.
May you be made strong with all the strength
that comes from his glorious power, and
may you be prepared to endure everything with patience,
while joyfully giving thanks to the Father,
who has enabled you to share in the inheritance
of the saints in the light.*

Colossians 1:9–12

The preceding chapters of this book focus on the prayers and scripture readings that comprise the Daily Prayer. This chapter introduces you to incorporating music, prayer beads, icons, candles, and other accoutrements into your daily prayer practices. These help engage your senses. When I use them, I am able to physically *experience* the prayers, not merely recite them.

Writing this chapter was somewhat intimidating for me at first. My concern was that I might leave out something helpful or overwhelm those who feel compelled to do all the things on a list. Rather than offer an entire catalog of music and auxiliary items or mention specific vendors, I curated a list of resources that I believe will have the staying power necessary to not be outdated as soon as we go to press. I also created a Daily Prayer resource page on my website: JoyHilley.com. I encourage you to check it for updates. If you find additional books or songs that are particularly helpful to you as you pray daily, please send me the links via the comment feature on my site. I would love to include them as resources for the benefit of others.

Using Music With the Daily Prayer

My earliest music memories are of listening to my dad's records of Mahalia Jackson and jazz trumpeters, hearing my mother play traditional hymns on the piano in her Southern Gospel style, and tuning in to Saturday radio programs for classical music. My music education was as eclectic as my religious education, and the following lists of recordings reflect that. I have included a range of styles to enrich your experience. Feel free to supplement them with your preferences.

Many of the scriptures used in the Daily Prayer have been set to music over the centuries. The music recording lists are arranged in the same order as the scriptures or prayers appear in the Daily Prayer: Jesus Prayer, Psalm 103, Psalm 23, The Lord's Prayer, and *Kyrie*. Like the supplemental prayers provided, I've made a *lagniappe* list of additional music that I occasionally include in my prayer time.

Using Art and Objects With the Daily Prayer

The early Christians used various symbols to represent their faith, including the fish and different types of crosses. In Greek, the word for fish is *ichthus*. Used as an acrostic, the word consists of the first letters of the phrase "Jesus Christ, Son of God, Savior" in Greek. At a time when Christians were tortured for their faith, the secret symbol could easily be drawn in the sand by one's foot, then as easily be erased after having done the work of identifying oneself as a follower of Christ.

When persecution forced the early Christians underground, they began to decorate the walls of the catacombs with pictures of Jesus, saints, and other symbols of the Christian faith. Fish, peacocks, anchors, shepherds, sheep, and myriad other things were drawn in these underground spaces, marking them as holy.

As Christianity spread throughout the Roman Empire and more Gentiles converted, icons that depicted the life of Christ, Old Testament themes, and saints were included in the visual expressions of faith. The development of stained glass introduced another opportunity for artists to portray the narrative of the Christian faith in worship spaces.

Almost from the beginning of the Church, the use of visual imagery has been debated. Acknowledging the Old Testament prohibition against worship of idols or images, the major point of contention is how those objects are used. Without retelling two thousand years of history, allow me to share my perspective.

We serve a God who values beauty. The vast array of colors in creation are but one hint at the visual feast God made available to us. Color, shape, texture, size, light, shadow—all help declare the glory of God!

We serve a God for whom beauty matters in worship. Even a cursory reading of Exodus 25–31 confirms that. Those chapters recount God's instructions to the Israelites for constructing the tabernacle—the place where they would meet him for sacrifice and worship on their exodus from Egyptian slavery. The finest metals, woods, linens, jewels, and other materials were designated for the tent of meeting. Requirements for using incense, candles, oil, water, and other sensory items were established. In the middle of the desert, even in a time of transition and extreme hardship, beauty was honored and celebrated.

For me, beauty matters as well—especially the beauty of creation and my surroundings. Engaging both sides of my brain and all my senses serves to enrich my daily prayer practice. To shut myself off from visual symbols, simply because I fear making them idols, is to ignore how each of us is capable of making an idol of anything or anyone.

Because beauty speaks to me and I find that symbols enhance my worship and prayer time, I have accumulated a collection of holy objects. They include a five-foot-long rosary made in Costa Rica, a very well-loved Sacred Heart of Jesus statue found in a dusty antique shop, prayer beads that I made from wood and clay, icons given as gifts to me, a beaded chaplet, crosses collected and gifted for the last thirty years, and beautiful candles.

Whether you embrace or forgo Christian symbols in your private worship and prayer time is a decision for you *and* the Spirit. Ask him what he wants you to do. Ask what will bring him honor and glory. Then do that.

Bible Translations

In the many Bible studies I've taught over the years, invariably the question is raised about which translation is best. Those who know me well know that I am willing to share my opinion when asked—and even on occasion when not asked! Before I give my opinion on this topic, however, let me give a brief overview of the development of the texts we now call the "Bible."

When you and I think of the Bible, we generally think of a unified document that contains sixty-six books. We readily accept that the Old Testament was translated from Hebrew and the New Testament was translated mostly from Greek. The Old Testament came to us almost completely intact from the Masoretes, a group of Jewish scribes and scholars who compiled it centuries before the birth of Christ. However, collecting reliable manuscripts for the New Testament was not as simple. More than 6,000 source texts were used—written by hand on a variety of materials, some surviving only as fragments.

As you can imagine, there are linguistic scholars who devote their entire lives to biblical textual history and criticism—to determine which of those thousands of pieces are the oldest and most reliable. Once the reliability of the documents is established, the task then becomes how to faithfully render ancient languages as modern languages.

One translation method, known as "formal equivalence," focuses on a word-for-word translation. The second translation method is known as "functional equivalence" or "dynamic equivalence" and focuses on phrases or sentences to get the "sense" of the text into the translation. The third process paraphrases the text. Usually the person or team paraphrasing the scripture begins with the text in their own native language, not with the original Hebrew or Greek, and rewrites it into common vernacular; it is not a translation.

Regardless of the method, a further decision must be made: who will translate or paraphrase the text? Will it be a single individual or will it be a committee? And if it's a committee, who will be on it? What theological, cultural, or ethnic biases might they bring to the task?

Another consideration is that language is not static. It changes and evolves over time. Words that meant a particular thing two hundred years ago—or even two decades ago—may now have a completely different meaning. For example, awful once meant "full or worthy of awe." Reading about the "awful majesty of God" from an ancient text then becomes a very different experience for modern readers who may not know or understand that the definition has changed since it was written.

Considering all these factors—and a few dozen others that I have not included here in the interest of time and space—I have selected the New Revised Standard Version (NRSV) for my personal reading. I use *The Harper Collins Study Bible NRSV* for study. It is a formal equivalence translation authored by a diverse committee of scholars. I often use other translations or paraphrases when I want to think about a particular passage in a new way or am looking for a particular rhythm of language when writing or speaking, but the NRSV is my translation of choice.

Whatever version of the Bible you choose, take time to do some research about it. Ask the Spirit to guide you. Then make an informed, thoughtful decision.

Jesus Prayer Recordings

Choirs of Annunciation Byzantine Catholic Church: *Theosis*
    "Jesus Prayer"

Jeff Johnson: *Lauds*
    "The Jesus Prayer"

Psalm 103 Recordings

Andraé Crouch: *Legends of Gospel*
    "Bless His Holy Name"

Esther Mui: *Scripture Songs for Worship*
    "Psalm 103:1–6 (Bless The Lord, O My Soul)"

PaTRAM Institute Male Choir: *Teach Me Thy Statutes*
    "Bless The Lord, O My Soul, Op. 40 No. 1"

Scott Cunningham Band: *Steadfast Love*
    "As the Heavens Are High (Psalm 103)"

The Prestonwood Choir: *Horizon*
    "103 (Bless the Lord)"

The Turtle Creek Chorale: *Psalms*
    "Psalm 103, Bless the Lord, My Soul"

Psalm 23 Recordings

Jon Foreman: *Limbs and Branches*
"The House of God, Forever"

Al Green: *Soul Survivor*
"23rd Psalm"

Whitney Houston: *The Preacher's Wife*
"The Lord Is My Shepherd (with Cissy Houston,
Hezekiah Walker, and The Love Fellowship Choir)"

Shane & Shane: *Psalms II*
"Psalm 23 (Surely Goodness, Surely Mercy)"

John Michael Talbot: *Master Collection (Vol. 1) The Quiet Side*
"Psalm 23 (The Lord Is My Shepherd)"

The Brooklyn Tabernacle Choir: *I Am Reminded (Live)*
"Psalm 23 (featuring Shane & Shane)"

The Cambridge Singers, John Rutter: *This Is the Day*
"Psalm 23, Op. 132, D. 706"

The Choir of King's College: *The Music of King's—
Choral Favourites From Cambridge*
"Psalm 23 (The Lord Is My Shepherd)"

Jason Upton: *Glimpse (Live)*
"Psalm 23 (Live)"

The Lord's Prayer Recordings

Andrea Bocelli: *Mi Navidad*
    "The Lord's Prayer (Mormon Tabernacle Choir)"
Doyle Dykes: *Gitarre 2000*
    "The Lord's Prayer"
Aretha Franklin: *One Lord, One Faith, One Baptism*
    "The Lord's Prayer (Live at New Bethel Baptist Church)"
Marvin Gaye: *The Master 1961–1984*
    "The Lord's Prayer (Live)"
Hillsong Worship: *There Is More (Live)*
    "The Lord's Prayer (Live)"
Mahalia Jackson: *The Essential Mahalia Jackson*
    "The Lord's Prayer (Live)"
Jubilee Worship: *Atmosphere Chapter 1*
    "The Lord's Prayer"
Sandra McCracken: *God's Highway*
    "The Lord's Prayer"
Page CXVI: *Hymns—Lullabies*
    "The Lord's Prayer"
Shane & Shane: *Everything Is Different*
    "The Lord's Prayer"
Richard Smallwood: *The Best of Richard Smallwood—
    The Millennium Collection*
    "The Lord's Prayer (Live)"

Kyrie Recordings

Federico Jusid, Orquesta Sinfónica de Budapest Eastconnection: *Isabel*
  "Kyrie"

The London Fox Taize Choir: *Jesus Remember Me—Taize Songs*
  "Kyrie Eleison (Lord, Have Mercy)"

Sandra McCracken: *Psalms*
  "Have Mercy"

Quire of Voyces: *The Latin Mass*
  "William Byrd—Kyrie"

The Sixteen: *Mass in B Minor (J. S. Bach) BWV 232*
  "Kyrie—Kyrie eleison II"

John Michael Talbot: *Living Water—50th*
  "Kyrie"

Chris Tomlin: *Never Lose Sight (Deluxe Edition)*
  "Kyrie Eleison (with Matt Maher, Matt Redman, Jason Ingram)"

Vineyard Worship: *Kyrie Eleison—Anchour Studio Sessions*
  "Kyrie Eleison"

Lagniappe Recordings

All Sons & Daughters: *Poets & Saints*
  "Rest In You"

Audrey Assad: *Inheritance*
  "Holy, Holy, Holy"

Thad Cockrell: *To Be Loved*
  "Oh To Be Loved"

Elevation Worship: *Paradoxology*
  "Paradoxology"

Elevation Worship: *Paradoxology*
  "Hallelujah Here Below (featuring Steffany Gretzinger)"

Josh Garrels: *The Light Came Down*
  "Hosanna"

Steffany Gretzinger: *Forever Amen*
  "No One Ever Cared For Me Like Jesus"

Sara Groves: *Abide With Me*
  "He's Always Been Faithful"

Christian-Pierre La Marca: *Cantus*
  "Ave Verum Corpus, K. 618"

Sandra McCracken: *God's Highway*
  "Steadfast"

The Cambridge Singers: *The Very Best of John Rutter*
  "The Lord Bless You and Keep You"

Westminster Choir: *O Magnum Mysterium (2018 Remaster)*
  "The Lord Bless You and Keep You (Peter Lutkin)"

Joy Hilley

Acknowledgments

For Joe, whose love and support have called me into my true self since 1984;

For Laura Catherine, who healed my heart in an instant in the hallway of a Chinese hotel;

For Jack, whose gentle, loving spirit is a balm to my soul;

For Chris, whose love and generosity have strengthened and encouraged me;

For Shawn, whose love and friendship are a gift from heaven and whose copy-editing skills are the finest in the land; and

For family members, friends, and ministers who have poured their wisdom and grace into my life,

I give thanks in every remembrance of you, constantly praying with joy in every one of my prayers for all of you.

CPSIA information can be obtained
at www.ICGtesting.com
Printed in the USA
LVHW042107040323
740950LV00001B/19